Long Ago and Today

by Quinn Douglas

Harcourt
SCHOOL PUBLISHERS

Printed in Mexico

ISBN 10: 0-15-350645-8
ISBN 13: 978-0-15-350645-1

Ordering Options
ISBN 10: 0-15-350599-0 (Grade 2 On-Level Collection)
ISBN 13: 978-0-15-350599-7 (Grade 2 On-Level Collection)
ISBN 10: 0-15-357826-2 (package of 5)
ISBN 13: 978-0-15-357826-7 (package of 5)

1 2 3 4 5 6 7 8 9 10   050   15 14 13 12 11 10 09 08 07 06

Imagine it is the year 1865. You are riding a bicycle made out of wood. It has steel wheels. The hard wheels bump along the road. The bicycle shakes badly, and so do you. The bicycle is called a "boneshaker".

Now imagine it is the year 1871.
You are riding a bicycle with a large
front wheel and a small back wheel.
You are sitting up really high. You
have to be careful that you don't
fall off!

The bicycle is called a "penny farthing". A penny was a large English coin and a farthing was a very small English coin. It was usually brave people who rode penny farthings!

In the 1870s, most girls learned to cook and sew. They did not often ride bicycles. The girls that did ride bicycles wore long pants called bloomers under their dresses.

Today, you can see many old bicycles in museums. Some people even collect them for fun.

The first bicycles made for children were very heavy. There were not many kinds to choose from.

Today, bicycles come in many shapes and sizes. Some of them are very expensive. Others do not cost much money at all. It can be hard to choose a bicycle!

Most bicycles today have gears. Gears make it easier or harder to pedal. Some bicycles have very light frames for racing. Other bicycles have strong frames and fat tires for riding on dirt tracks.

In the 1950s, families began to ride bicycles to keep fit and for fun. Special bicycle trails were built in some parks and on roads. Bicycle riding became more and more popular.

Today, people wear special things to protect their heads, arms, and legs. There are laws in many states that say that bicycle riders must wear helmets. It is important that all riders know the bicycle rules where they live.

Some places have bicycle safety classes for children. They are usually held in parking lots. Streets are marked on the ground with chalk. Children ride around the chalk streets and learn to ride safely.

Long ago, people played bicycle board games. Today, people enjoy playing bicycle video games. Bicycles are a favorite pastime for many people around the world.